Debunking the Myths of Forgive-And-Forget

by
Kay Bruner

Contents

Forgiveness: the Christian F word, or rest for your soul?

There are certain words that I hate to use because they're loaded with terrible connotations.

"Forgiveness" is one of those words.

Don't get me wrong. I think forgiveness can be a wonderful, freeing thing.

It's just that people have so often been told to "forgive" in a way that is anything but wonderful and freeing.

I think we've used "forgive" as a way to shut people up, frankly. We tell other people to forgive because we can't deal with their reality. We get uncomfortable with the terrible pain of another person, and to escape it, we say, "Forgive." Then we can check our "I gave good spiritual advice" box and walk away.

We slap each other with the "Christian F word" and think we've done a good day's work, leaving behind a victim now staggering under yet another weight. They've got the pain they started with, and we've just loaded on guilt and shame, as we imply that their problems are their fault since they haven't forgiven properly.

Because of all the baggage around forgiveness, I never, ever tell my clients they have to forgive anybody. But they ask me about it anyway.

"What about forgiveness?" they'll ask. Because terrible

things have happened to them, often repeatedly.

What are we supposed to do with these awful things? The Bible says 70 times 7, and we've tried to forgive, but it doesn't seem to be helping like we'd hoped. We've tried to be nice, but the other person still flies into a rage. We've tried to forget about it, but we still flinch at sudden moves. How do we get past it?

We've tried forgiving and forgetting, but we're still getting knocked around, 70 times 7. It hurts. It keeps on hurting.

We've heard great stories about forgiveness from other people, all about freedom and relief and release. We'd like to have freedom and relief. We really would. We long for it. We really do.

It's just a whole lot more complicated than we'd anticipated, and the advice we've gotten about forgiveness feels more like a bigger burden than any kind of relief.

And here, in the privacy of the therapy room, we're willing to say that the easy answers about forgiveness don't work, and we need something better.

Here's the good news: Jesus offers us something far better than yet another burden to bear.

"Come unto me, all ye that labor and are heavy laden, and I will give you rest. Take my yoke upon you, and learn of me; for I am meek and lowly in heart: and ye shall find rest unto your souls. For my yoke is easy, and my burden is light."

Matthew 11:28-30, KJV

"The Spirit of the Lord is on me, because he has anointed me to proclaim good news to the poor. He has sent me to proclaim freedom for the prisoners and recovery of sight for the blind, to set the oppressed free, to proclaim the year of the Lord's favor."

Luke 4:18,19, NIV

Whenever our practice of forgiveness brings a burden onto victims, our practice is wrong.

Wherever our practice of forgiveness is anything less than good news to victims, it is a lie.

Wherever our practice of forgiveness brings bondage and blindness, secrecy, silence and oppression, it is way out of line with the Lord's favor.

And that's where we need to re-examine our understanding of forgiveness, so that it brings rest to our souls, like Jesus intended for it to do.

I think our misunderstandings about forgiveness center around six forgiveness myths that I hope to debunk:

Forgiveness is quick and easy

Forgiveness makes me a victim

Forgiveness is a magic wand

Forgiveness means I can't confront

Forgiveness restores the relationship automatically

Forgiveness requires restoration of the relationship

My hope is that, as we debunk these myths, we'll find ourselves finally able to really, truly forgive and live in the rest and freedom that Jesus promises.

Myth #1: Forgiveness is quick and easy

Lots of us, let's just go ahead and admit it, have been seduced by IKEA furniture. We're wandering through Furniture Wonderland. It's all so stylish, so inexpensive, and so easy to transport in those great flat-pack boxes. We get to locate the box in the warehouse, which is a cool adventure. Even the instructions are adorable, with that pudgy little cartoon person always smiling away. And the whole store smells like cinnamon buns. What could be better?

But once we've lugged it home, and we start to put the thing together, reality bites. Maybe for some people, the assembly is as easy as the cartoon guy makes it look, but for me, it's just not that way. Of all the things that happen to me while trying to assemble IKEA furniture, smiling is not one of them.

Forgiveness, as a floor model, is like that to me. I'm told that it's wonderful, and right, and good, and I want things like that in my life.

The instructions look really simple: "Say you're sorry." "Say I forgive you." "Hug your brother."

Those instructions worked pretty well when I was six years old, and my biggest problem was sharing the toys in the sandbox. But as I got older and the problems got more complicated, forgiveness got a lot more complex, too. I found myself trying to follow the directions, only to end up lost and confused.

A parable about forgiveness

Then Peter came to him and asked, "Lord, how often should I forgive someone who sins against me? Seven times?"

"No, not seven times," Jesus replied, "but seventy times seven!

"Therefore, the Kingdom of Heaven can be compared to a king who decided to bring his accounts up to date with servants who had borrowed money from him. In the process, one of his debtors was brought in who owed him millions of dollars. He couldn't pay, so his master ordered that he be sold--along with his wife, his children, and everything he owned--to pay the debt.

"But the man fell down before his master and begged him, 'Please, be patient with me, and I will pay it all.' Then his master was filled with pity for him, and he released him and forgave his debt.

"But when the man left the king, he went to a fellow servant who owed him a few thousand dollars. He grabbed him by the throat and demanded instant payment.

"His fellow servant fell down before him and begged for a little more time. 'Be patient with me, and I will pay it,' he pleaded. But his creditor wouldn't wait. He had the man arrested and put in prison until the debt could be paid in full.

"When some of the other servants saw this, they were very upset. They went to the king and told him everything that had happened. Then the king called in the man he had forgiven and said, 'You evil servant! I forgave you that tremendous debt because you pleaded with me. Shouldn't you have mercy on your fellow servant, just as I had mercy on you?'

"Then the angry king sent the man to prison to be tortured until he had paid his entire debt.

"That's what my heavenly Father will do to you if you refuse to forgive your brothers and sisters from your heart."

When Jesus had finished saying these things, he left Galilee and went down to the region of Judea east of the Jordan River. Large crowds followed him there, and he healed their sick.

Matthew 18:21-19:2, New Living Translation

In this parable, we find Jesus at the height of his teaching career. He's traveling the countryside, feeding the hungry, healing the sick, raising the dead, and answering a list of FAQ's from the disciples as they all walk along. The disciples have a lot of questions about how to live out their relationship with God in the real world, and Jesus spends a lot of time answering those questions, like this one from Peter:

"How many times should I forgive someone who keeps doing the same thing over and over? Seven times?"

Jesus famously says, "Seventy times seven." Some translations say seventy-seven times. Either way, it's a big number. Honestly? An impossible number. Then Jesus tells the parable: a guy who owes millions has that huge debt forgiven. Then he turns around and throws somebody else in jail for owing him seven cents or seventy-seven cents or seventy-times-seven cents.

Any way you slice it, seven cents or seventy-seven cents or seventy-times-seven cents is nowhere near millions. When you compare the big debt of millions to this other amount, the numbers just don't add up. It seems like forgiveness is no big deal, right?

Forgive and don't worry about that minor loss. That seems to be the message.

What's more, the guy who owes millions seems to have a pretty serious problem with destructive entitlement. He gets forgiven this huge thing, but he can't even let go of this one little thing.

Forgive and don't be an ungrateful jerk. That seems to be the message.

Finally, the angry king sends the jerk to prison to be tortured until he can pay back the millions, and that's what will happen to us if we don't forgive.

Forgive or else you'll be tortured. That seems to be the message.

The instructions seem so simple and straightforward. They've been around for thousands of years. Why do we still have questions about this? Well, because we've tried it the easy way, and, like all those so-simple IKEA instruction booklets, the easy way left us lost and confused.

Reflect

When you hear the word "forgive," whose face comes into your mind?

What are the most difficult offenses that you have to forgive?

What problems have you encountered when you try to forgive these difficult things?

A personal story

My husband, Andy, used to have a pretty serious internet pornography habit. He managed to hide it from me for six years, but finally his behavior became more and more obvious to me, until I had to admit to myself that something was wrong. When I woke up, once again, in the middle of the night, to find him, once again, at the computer, I had to ask, "Are you looking at pornography?" And he said, "Yes, I am."

He was terribly sorry for what he had been doing, he said. He would never do it again, he said.

So I did what I knew to do. I listened to what he had to say. I didn't ask too many questions. I was as forgiving as I knew how to be. I didn't make a big deal about it, really. I was sad, but I didn't let myself be angry. I just tried to forgive and forget.

A few months later, he confessed to looking at pornography again. This time I remember saying to him, "I don't think this is fair. You get to keep doing this thing, telling me you just can't help it, and I have to keep forgiving you. I don't like this at all."

After that, he didn't confess any more. He hid it again for

several months, until the whole thing finally came out. Did I mention that we were missionaries at the time? And did you know that missionary organizations frown on pornography use? Those circumstances being true, our mission organization sent us back from overseas to the States, and then they spent several months figuring out what to do with us.

So there I was, with my life in pieces around me, trying to figure out what it meant to forgive my husband in the real world. My challenges were these:

The problem was a real problem, not just me being easily offended.

The problem was so severe that we were in danger of losing our marriage over it.

Andy couldn't or wouldn't stop the problem.

Everything I knew about forgiving my husband ended up enabling his sin.

It really was seventy times seven, and that was a big, bad, soul-crushing number—even though I knew God had forgiven many more sins in me. The "compare-my-sin-to-your-sin" tactic didn't help at all.

My understanding of forgiveness from childhood meant: be nice, overlook it, forget it, move on. But that model of forgiveness just wasn't adequate when I came up against something that I knew for sure was wrong, and that threatened to undo my whole world. In fact, if I kept forgiving like I did in the sandbox, Andy and I were going to end up in a bigger and bigger mess.

Forgiveness is not quick and easy. It's just not true in the real world.

Reflect

Name a problem that's a real problem, and not just you being easily offended.

What have you tried in terms of forgiveness so far?

What frustrations or difficulties are you facing as you try to forgive?

Myth #2: Forgiveness makes me a victim

I read how-to manuals on forgiveness. I read memoirs of people who had survived terrible crimes and lived to forgive. I went to workshops on peacemaking. I ploughed through whatever I could find, of what the Bible and Christians have to say about forgiveness. At the same time, I was reading *Boundaries* by Henry Cloud and John Townsend. I knew I needed boundaries to be healthy, but I didn't know how to put boundaries and forgiveness together.

I continued to struggle with the seemingly easy answer that Jesus gives to Peter: "Seventy times seven." It seemed like Jesus was telling Peter to have no boundaries, overlook sin, and be an enabler. If I did that, I was going to keep being a victim, and Andy was going to keep on sinning without restraint. I knew that couldn't be right. It was confusing.

Eventually, I did what my Bible professors told me to do in college: I read the context of the parable. And that turned out to be remarkably clarifying. Instead of starting in verse 21 of Matthew 18, I went all the way back to the beginning of the chapter. Here's what it says:

About that time the disciples came to Jesus and asked, "Who is greatest in the Kingdom of Heaven?"

Jesus called a little child to him and put the child among them. Then he said, "I tell you the truth, unless you turn from your sins and become like little children, you will never get into the Kingdom of Heaven. So anyone who becomes as humble as this little child is the greatest in the Kingdom of Heaven.

"And anyone who welcomes a little child like this on my behalf is welcoming me. But if you cause one of these little ones who trusts in me to fall into sin, it would be better for you to have a large millstone tied around your neck and be drowned in the depths of the sea.

"What sorrow awaits the world, because it tempts people to sin. Temptations are inevitable, but what sorrow awaits the person who does the tempting. So if your hand or foot causes you to sin, cut it off and throw it away. It's better to enter eternal life with only one hand or one foot than to be thrown into eternal fire with both of your hands and feet. And if your eye causes you to sin, gouge it out and throw it away. It's better to enter eternal life with only one eye than to have two eyes and be thrown into the fire of hell.

"Beware that you don't look down on any of these little ones. For I tell you that in heaven their angels are always in the presence of my heavenly Father.

"If a man has a hundred sheep and one of them wanders away, what will he do? Won't he leave the ninety-nine others on the hills and go out to search for the one that is lost? And if he finds it, I tell you the truth, he will rejoice over it more than over the ninety-nine that didn't wander away! In the same way, it is not my heavenly Father's will that even one of these little ones should perish.

Matthew 18:1-14 NLT

At the beginning of the chapter, the disciples ask this question, "Who's the greatest?"

Just as there is a literary context for the 70 x 7 parable, there is a historical context for this question.

The disciples were living under the rule of Herod the Great, who was in turn under the rule of Rome. As a "client king," Herod paid tribute to Rome, and in return, Rome allowed the Jews to keep their religious practices and a certain amount of freedom. Along with paying tribute to Rome, Herod also outlaid enormous expenditures as he rebuilt the Temple, turning it into a spectacular religious showpiece, and a tourist attraction.

One scholar has this to say: "The way to think of the Temple with Herod's vision, is to think almost of an airport as much as a of a church or something like that. He created architecturally a space that could accommodate an enormous number of pilgrims and tourists and interested others."[1]

The disciples are dealing with Roman occupation, and a king who's creating a religious DisneyTemple in Jerusalem. Where does the money come from for these ventures? Taxes. Who pays these taxes? The disciples and other common people. It's not an especially happy to time to a common person in Judea.

So, there the disciples were one fine day, out trying to catch enough fish to pay their taxes so Herod could pay Rome and refurbish his tourist trap. Jesus comes by, performing miracles and gathering crowds of followers, and invites the disciples to come with him. It must have been their fondest dream-come-true to meet Jesus, with his miracles and enormous popularity. Naturally, in their minds, he would use all that miraculous power and popularity to remove hateful Herod and his Romans from power, and to bring in his own kingdom.

It's important to note that every ruler at the time said they were a deity. It was normal at that time to identify your own kingdom as a heavenly kingdom. (That's exactly what Herod was doing with his Temple refurbishing project, and it helps us understand why Jesus got so angry when he went there. Matthew chapter 21 tells that story.) Jesus could call his kingdom "the Kingdom of Heaven" all he wanted, and the disciples still wouldn't get it. In the disciples' minds, when Jesus' "Kingdom of Heaven" came, the disciples would be right there with him as he defeated the current kingdoms of Herod and Caesar. When that happened, being the greatest in the kingdom would be—well, the greatest. So this is the question they ask.

In response to their question, though, Jesus gives this mind-bending answer. He calls a little child into their circle and says, "Turn from your sins and become like little children. If you want to be great in the Kingdom of Heaven, be like this child."

What the disciples don't understand is this: Jesus is not interested in being Herod 2.0. He's not interested in taking power, or teaching the disciples how to take power. Why?

Because power separates.

The powerful from the powerless. The one-up from the

one-down. The rich from the poor. The victim from the oppressor. The greatest in the kingdom from the less-great.

And separating one group from another is not what God was doing when he sent Jesus into the world.

As the apostle Paul would write just a few years later, **God was reconciling the world to himself through Jesus.** (I Corinthians 5:19)

Jesus would then pass along the ministry of reconciliation to his disciples—and eventually, to you and me. In order to become "ministers of reconciliation", the disciples (and we) have to drop this idea that power is the way to go, because power inherently separates. It cannot reconcile. And so, when they ask this question about who will be greatest, Jesus lets them know they're on the wrong track, by laying out an entirely different way of dealing with the world: become like a child.

I think Jesus is telling us something like this:

Instead of being dominant seekers after power, we are to become childlike receivers of a tough, passionate, assertive, sacrificial Love that flows from our Father, to us, and then into the rest of the world.

Having said that we're to become like little children, why does Jesus then start talking about abused children and lost sheep? I think he's addressing this underlying issue that the disciples live with, day in and day out: injustice. **He wants the disciples to understand that "like a child" doesn't mean "like a victim."**

16

"But if you cause one of these little ones who trusts in me to fall into sin, it would be better for you to have a large millstone tied around your neck and be drowned in the depths of the sea.

"What sorrow awaits the world, because it tempts people to sin. Temptations are inevitable, but what sorrow awaits the person who does the tempting. So if your hand or foot causes you to sin, cut it off and throw it away. It's better to enter eternal life with only one hand or one foot than to be thrown into eternal fire with both of your hands and feet. And if your eye causes you to sin, gouge it out and throw it away. It's better to enter eternal life with only one eye than to have two eyes and be thrown into the fire of hell."

Mark 9:42 NLT

Jesus tells us that he cares passionately about the abandoned, the poor, the downtrodden. Injustice, as Jesus talks about it, is not something to put up with, or to quickly "forgive and forget." Injustice is something to be resisted and corrected and dealt with. When we find ourselves confronted with injustice, we ought to take the strongest possible steps to stop it, chopping off our own hands and feet if they lead us into victimizing others. Furthermore, the Great Shepherd seeks out the victims of injustice, to find them and gently carry them home.

The message to the disciples goes something like this:

Power might turn you into the person at the top of the heap, and that seems like the answer when you've been victimized. But power won't meet the needs of your heart. It won't heal your pain and reconcile you to God

and each other. Only Love can do that, and Love won't leave you a victim.

What a potent message to us, as we live out the work of reconciliation in the world today, and as we consider what forgiveness really means.

Seizing power over others will get us nowhere in the end. No matter how hard we hold on to our anger, no matter how effectively we wield it against others, that will never heal our broken hearts. Only Love can heal us. And Love has promised never to leave us, never to forsake us, and to work all things together for good. (Deuteronomy 31:6, Hebrews 13:5, Romans 8:28)

In the context of the Love of God, poured out for us and carrying us every step of every day, we undertake the work of forgiveness.

Reflect

What is your experience with the promises that Love will never leave us, never forsake us, and work all things together for good?

How has that been true or false in your life?

When have you felt abandoned?

When have you felt that events were absolutely destructive, rather than working together for good?

How does your experience contribute to your feelings as

18

you read this book right now?

Right now, identify your emotions. Are you sad, mad, or scared?

Assertiveness and forgiveness

Next, Jesus takes the power discussion out of the theoretical world of innocent children and fluffy lambs, and tells the disciples what to do when injustice visits *their own lives*. Jesus knows that bad people are going to happen to his disciples. What should they do when those bad people happen to them?

Forgive and forget?

Pretend it was no big deal?

Look for opportunities to grab power, and get an eye for an eye and a tooth for a tooth?

None of the above. Jesus carefully outlines a process for dealing with injustice, and it has nothing to do with seizing power over others, or living as a silent victim. Instead of swinging back and forth on the power paradigm between passive and aggressive, *Jesus offers us a different way: assertiveness and forgiveness.* Assertiveness and forgiveness is the way Love works for the good of both parties, to make a way for healing and reconciliation.

"If another believer sins against you, go privately and point out the fault. If the other person listens and confesses it, you have won that person back. But if you are unsuccessful, take one or two others with you and go back again, so that everything you say may be confirmed

by two or three witnesses. If that person still refuses to listen, take your case to the church. If the church decides you are right, but the other person won't accept it, treat that person as a pagan or a corrupt tax collector."

Matthew 18:15-17, NLT

Jesus tells the disciples to go to the offender alone, and talk to him about the sin. Pursue reconciliation with all your heart. If that doesn't work, bring along a witness, he says. Then take it to the church for judgment, and ultimately, treat the person "as a pagan" if they don't listen to the church.

There's a lot of discussion out there in the Christian world about what the phrase "as a pagan" means, but to me it would just be something like this: "Our ideas of reality don't mesh, and until we're able to agree, we can't have a close relationship." I don't think Jesus is telling us to hate people or treat them badly. Just recognize reality for what it is and allow others to have their free will, while we take responsibility for our own free will and practice appropriate boundaries.

The message I hear from Jesus is this: "You matter to me. You're not the victim in that old power paradigm. You're my precious child. Speak up. Get others to help you, if needed. Establish boundaries, and hold them firmly. When you're out of assertive options, let the other person go, if they aren't prepared to be in a healthy relationship." That's a robust statement about our value as individuals, and our responsibility to live assertively and seek justice— and not just for helpless others, but for ourselves as well.

Then--after all this teaching about our inherent value, God's protective love, and our responsibility to operate with assertiveness--finally, the text picks up with our seventy-times-seven parable. Peter thinks about that one person who just never gets it. That one person who keeps doing the same thing over and over, no matter what. He asks the next logical question: "What about this person who won't repent? How many times do I need to forgive him, exactly?"

"No, not seven times," Jesus replied, "but seventy times seven!

"Therefore, the Kingdom of Heaven can be compared to a king who decided to bring his accounts up to date with servants who had borrowed money from him. In the process, one of his debtors was brought in who owed him millions of dollars. He couldn't pay, so his master ordered that he be sold--along with his wife, his children, and everything he owned--to pay the debt.

"But the man fell down before his master and begged him, 'Please, be patient with me, and I will pay it all.' Then his master was filled with pity for him, and he released him and forgave his debt.

"But when the man left the king, he went to a fellow servant who owed him a few thousand dollars. He grabbed him by the throat and demanded instant payment.

"His fellow servant fell down before him and begged for a little more time. 'Be patient with me, and I will pay it,' he pleaded. But his creditor wouldn't wait. He had the man arrested and put in prison until the debt could be paid in full.

"When some of the other servants saw this, they were very upset. They went to the king and told him everything that had happened. Then the king called in the man he had forgiven and said, 'You evil servant! I forgave you that tremendous debt because you pleaded with me. Shouldn't you have mercy on your fellow servant, just as I had mercy on you?'

"Then the angry king sent the man to prison to be tortured until he had paid his entire debt.

"That's what my heavenly Father will do to you if you refuse to forgive your brothers and sisters from your heart."

When Jesus had finished saying these things, he left Galilee and went down to the region of Judea east of the Jordan River. Large crowds followed him there, and he healed their sick.

Matthew 18:21-19:2, NLT

Here's what I hear Jesus saying to Peter in the end: "You're right. You can't control what other people are going to do. **Remember, we don't live in the power paradigm. We live as receivers and givers of Love, dedicated to offering reconciliation, not insisting on control.** After you've confronted the person, and pursued justice, sadly, that person may not choose reconciliation. Eventually, you might just have to forgive, seventy times seven. But guess what, you have more resources than you've ever explored. Stop obsessing about what this one person owes you, and revel in all the riches of the Kingdom. Once you do that, that old debt might not matter quite as much. But let me tell you, if you're so determined to pursue what that one person owes you, you're going to turn your back on the treasure, and you'll end up miserable. That's how it works. You've got free will. You choose."

Jesus tells it like it is. It's not a threat, just a reality check. This is the truth we have to face: when we keep trying to get back what that person owes us, we turn our backs on all the wealth God has for us, and that has consequences in our own lives. However, *when we remember that our whole lives are held in the context of value, love, and assertiveness,* we can make other choices. When we know that there is enough for us, we don't need what that other person has. Within that framework, we are finally able to forgive from a position of emotional and spiritual safety.

The servant in the parable is forgiven a huge debt, but he's so used to living like he needs to scrape every last penny up off the sidewalk that he just can't wrap his head around letting go of what the other guy owes him. Instead of enjoying the immense wealth he's received, he obsesses over this one thing he can't force the other guy to give him.

And we do that, too. For some of us, living like a victim is all we know. Because we've been powerless, we can only imagine gaining power to use over others. We're so used to being desperate for what That One Person owes us that we keep ourselves locked up trying to choke that last 77 cents out of him.

We only know how to grapple with poverty and power. We don't know how to live in the wealth of belovedness.

But this is the radical offering I hear Jesus making to me: "You don't need what he's got. Remember the power paradigm can't heal you. I've got way more Love than you can possibly imagine. Take what I'm offering, and walk out of the cage."

Forgiveness is not another burden for us.

It's the way to live free and clear, but we've got to take our hands off the other person's throat in order to receive the gift of freedom.

Archbishop Desmond Tutu, who lived through the horrors of apartheid South Africa, and then headed the country's council on truth and reconciliation, puts it this way: "You can choose forgiveness or revenge, but revenge is always costly. Choosing forgiveness rather than retaliation ultimately serves to make you a stronger and freer person. Peace always comes to those who choose to forgive."

Reading the forgiveness parable in its context empowers me in a whole new way. I no longer think that I just have to put up with anything anybody wants to do to me, seventy times seven. I'm not a helpless victim any more. Instead, I'm the Beloved of Jesus. When someone sins against me, Jesus is angry. When I'm left scared and alone, Jesus is coming to rescue me. When someone sins against me, I have value and a voice and there's an assertive process for me to pursue. Out of all those resources, out of all that support, out of all that love that's available to me, I can forgive the debt that is owed to me. Maybe even seventy times seven.

Forgiveness, it turns out, is not about being a powerless victim, a doormat to the world.

24

Instead, it is part of an assertive life of peace and whole-ness.

Reflect

Think about a time when you felt unable to control your circumstances.

How does it feel to be a victim? How do you tend to respond during times like that?

How does God seem to feel about you and respond to you during those times?

Think about a time when you seized power and retaliation.

How did that experience mark your life? How did it impact those around you?

Myth #3: Forgiveness condones abuse

Too many times, forgiveness is treated like a magic wand that will somehow overcome the free will of another person and miraculously make deep problems disappear. Hopefully, it's clear by now that Jesus feels intensely protective toward those who are the victims of abuse and he understands that real problems need to be addressed with real solutions. However, since the church has historically been less clear than Jesus about this, I think we need to address this issue directly.

I can't tell you how many times I hear from women, "I told my pastor/Christian counselor/friend about the abuse, and they told me to pray and forgive and submit, so that my husband could be won without a word."

Apparently there are lots of Christians who feel comfortable giving that kind of advice to victims of abuse, but in light of Jesus' words about lopping off body parts, gouging out eyes, and millstones in the deepest part of the sea, I am not one of those Christians.

I am one of the ones who follow this command of Jesus: *"If he refuses to repent, treat him as a pagan."* (Matthew 18:17 NLT)

Someone who abuses his wife and/or children in any way—physically, emotionally, verbally, sexually--is acting like a pagan. Whenever behavior moves past normal conflict and into abuse, the offender has made his choice. If he refuses to repent, let him live with the consequences he has chosen.

26

Often, we see abusive, adulterous, addicted people being caught and immediately saying, "I made a terrible mistake, and I repent." While there's nothing wrong with this statement, these words are only words. Sometimes words are a good start toward repentance, and other times, they're just words on the way to more bad choices. The only way we can tell the difference between the two is by observing the individual's behavior over time.

True repentance means CHANGE. Change, in the serious cases we're thinking about here, does not happen easily or overnight. Extensive habits of thought, word, and belief need to be acknowledged, unraveled, and healed in the offender's life. Often, the offender has an immense wall of defense mechanisms in place that have allowed him to continue in his abusive habits. Those defense mechanisms are full of lies he's believed, and blame he's placed on his victims. That whole toxic structure has to be challenged and torn down, before healthy new thoughts and beliefs can grow into place. That is a long and painful process for the offender.

There is no way we know for sure if that person has changed until we see their life, and that generally takes a great deal of hard work on the offender's part, over time. Even then, even if the offender changes, the relationship may be too damaged for restoration. I'll address this is greater detail later on.

For now, though, hear this: you are infinitely precious and valuable to God. He does not intend for you to be abused or mistreated. In fact, it makes him violently angry just thinking about it, remember? He intends to rescue, protect, shelter, and heal you. You can participate in that healing by finding support with safe people while you decide how to create healthy boundaries, and live a life that reflects how beloved you are to God.

Forgiveness is not a magic wand that makes abuse or addiction or adultery disappear.

Reflect

Has the "magic wand" approach ever been used on you?

How did that experience impact you?

Have you used the "magic wand" on others? How might they have been impacted?

Myth #4: Forgiveness means I can't confront

"If another believer sins against you, go privately and point out the fault. If the other person listens and confesses it, you have won that person back. But if you are unsuccessful, take one or two others with you and go back again, so that everything you say may be confirmed by two or three witnesses. If that person still refuses to listen, take your case to the church. If the church decides you are right, but the other person won't accept it, treat that person as a pagan or a corrupt tax collector."

Matthew 18:15-17, NLT

The Bible tells us to forgive, and it tells us to confront. These sometimes seem like separate processes: forgiveness is nice, confrontation is mean. I think, however, that they are interrelated relationship skills that need to be talked about together. I don't think you can forgive without confronting what's wrong. Confrontation is often misunderstood, though, just like forgiveness.

When I was in junior high, a member of our extended family attended a Bible-teaching conference where the above passage was apparently a main topic of exhortation. When our relative returned home, other members of the family were soon deluged with letters, detailing all the faults they had committed against this family member, since early childhood. Needless to say, this did not promote confession and reconciliation, since most of the accused could not remember the incidents at all. The outcome was simply amazement that this person had the capacity to hold grudges for so many decades. They also took caution against being too closely engaged with the person in the future.

When we take the forgiveness parable out of context, it's overly simplistic and doesn't work in the real world. We need the context to make sense of it, and to understand the passionate heart of justice and mercy that can bring us to a place of true forgiveness.

The same goes for these verses about confrontation. Jesus has just been talking about people gouging out eyes and hacking off limbs before they consider sinning against one of his children. Clearly, Jesus is talking about severe problems and not who took the red wagon away from whom, back in the day. There are some questions we need to ask ourselves, before we "confront the sin" of another person.

Question 1: Is this issue not a sin, but a simple difference?

An awful lot of the things we get offended about are *simply differences of opinion or dissimilarities of preference*. I want to have lunch every week, while my friend wants to have lunch once a month. My friend votes Republican and I'm a Yellow Dog Democrat. I might not like these differences, but they are hardly sins against me.

Before we ever go confront someone about how they've hurt us, and how wrong they are, we first have to ask ourselves: *is it really a sin against me? Or did the person just do something I don't like?* Having a difference of opinion, even about very important issues, is not a sin. It's just a difference of opinion.

Some of us find it very challenging to deal with differences, but that is our own problem, not the other person's. Our

30

emotions are things for us to face up to, and deal with, in our own hearts.

We can go ahead and have a discussion about those differences if we want, but we're not confronting sin. We're just talking about differences.

Question 2: Is some other factor making me especially reactive?

Here's another question we have to ask ourselves before confronting: *are we especially reactive to this particular situation as a result of larger distress in our lives?* When we feel powerless, when we feel victimized, we often try to seize emotional power by pointing out others' faults. In reality, though, that person's actions may be a drop in the bucket of pain that we carry. This person I'm feeling so compelled to straighten out may just be the only person close enough to take a swipe at, when my grievance is really with larger, more painful circumstances.

Guess what? Jesus talks about this very thing in Matthew 7. He's winding down the Sermon on the Mount, when he says:

"Stop judging others, and you will not be judged. For others will treat you as you treat them. Whatever measure you use in judging others, it will be used to measure how you are judged. And why worry about a speck in your friend's eye when you have a log in your own? **How can you think of saying, 'Let me help you get rid of that speck in your eye' when you have a log in your own eye?** *Hypocrite! First get rid of the log from your own eye; then perhaps you will see well enough to*

deal with the speck in your friend's eye."

Matthew 7:1-5, NLT

We have to consider our own pain, our own circumstances—the log in our own eye--before we start confronting others about their stuff. We don't have to be perfectly sinless to confront, otherwise we'd never be able to do go and talk to the person who has sinned against us, like Jesus tells us to do in Matthew 18. But he's telling us, here in Matthew 7, to check our own hearts, before we go flinging our pain and self-righteous anger everywhere. If we are constantly emotional about every single speck in every single eye for a 50-mile radius, then maybe—just maybe—the problem is not just the specks. Maybe it's my log. Maybe I've got something to work on, before I try to work on everybody else.

Question 3: Is this any of my business?

Before I confront someone, I have to ask myself: *is this even my business?* The Matthew 18 forgiveness parable is not about marching around, randomly telling people that they are in sin.

First of all, it's just not our job to straighten everybody else out. There is a Holy Spirit, and that Holy Spirit is, I can confidently say, not you or me.

Second, from the context, this particular passage is about a serious transgression *against me personally*. It's my business if the offense is against me personally, and it's damaging the relationship between me and the offender. If the offense is not against me personally, then it might be one of those cases that the old Polish proverb talks about: not my circus, not my monkeys.

Question 4: Is this an issue for law enforcement, rather than the church?

Finally, none of these scriptures are about covering up criminal activity. There have been far too many cases (one would be too many) where people did not report known child abuse within a Christian group, instead choosing to "confront the brother," who magically repented and was restored to fellowship instantly.

If someone is abusing a child, an elderly person, or a person with disabilities, these activities are criminal and should be reported to the police by anyone who has knowledge of the events.

In the case of domestic violence, by one adult against another, I think it's wise to report that to the police as well, although it is the victim's choice and responsibility to do so. I would adamantly discourage a woman from confronting her abuser in some misguided attempt to "be scriptural." The abuser has already proven that he is physically dangerous, and I think it's best to allow law enforcement officials to handle physically dangerous people who are, once again, breaking the law.

We must never, ever misuse the concept of "Christian confrontation" to make the church a haven for abuse.

What is confrontation for, anyway?

So this kind of confrontation is not something to undertake lightly, it's not about us taking our emotions out on others, it's not about randomly sharing the news with people that they're bad, and it's not about protecting abusers or criminals. What, then, is this confrontation for, in the real world?

Let's remember what Jesus is talking about here: "if your brother sins against you." This sounds like someone close to you, and it sounds like the fault is a real fault. The relationship is under serious threat. To me, those are the times you confront the person seriously.

It's important to understand that the hope of confrontation is to restore the relationship. Remember, we've been given the ministry of reconciliation. Everything needs to fit within that framework. We can't force others to be reconciled, but we can offer reconciliation.

Too often, we think that "confront" is a hit-and-run, where we throw a giant bomb of all our offenses at the other person and take off before it can explode on us. In fact, "confront" means that you turn toward, you engage. Seen this way, confrontation is part of a process toward reconciliation. "Confront" means that you're willing to talk through the hard things, in an effort to restore a relationship. You hope and pray that the other person wants to participate. That's the process Jesus describes in Matthew 18. Confront, bring another person and try again, take it to the church, and then let go if the person refuses to hear it.

Andy's pornography addiction was a very serious threat

to our marriage. If Andy and I didn't confront that issue and resolve it, our family was going to fall apart. There was nothing I would have liked better than to overlook it and pretend it wasn't happening, but that wasn't possible. Confronting that sin was incredibly difficult and painful for both of us. I've often said it was like crawling over broken glass. It was tough, it was challenging, it changed us completely, but we won the relationship back, and I would crawl back over all that broken glass again to get where we are now. Much of what I believe about forgiveness now, I learned during those weeks and months and years of hard relationship work.

I understand now that Jesus is outraged when I'm victimized. I understand that he's not going to leave me alone and afraid someplace. He's coming for me, to carry me home. I understand that it's my job to stand up against sin when it comes against me, and work for the restoration of the relationship. I'll overlook when I need to, and I'll confront if I have to. Ultimately, I can release the relationship if it cannot be reconciled, because Jesus has way more for me than this person ever could.

Reflect

Where has injustice visited your life?

How do you feel, when you think about being assertive against injustice in your own life?

What fears arise when you think of being assertive?

How was assertiveness viewed in your family of origin?

Were there different rules for men and women when it came to assertiveness?

Have you ever been the victim of a hit-and-run confrontation? What was the result?

Have you ever been the perpetrator in a hit-and-run confrontation? What happened?

Myth #5: Forgiveness restores the relationship automatically

Aside from scriptural misunderstandings about forgiveness, I think we've got a lot of practical misunderstandings as well. Here are some of the misunderstandings I've had to work through.

I expected that when I forgave the person, I would immediately stop feeling pain and sadness and anger.

I expected that when I forgave the person, he would immediately stop doing the bad thing.

Above all else, I expected that if I forgave the person, the relationship would automatically be restored.

Once I worked through what scripture says, and learned to have boundaries and be assertive around forgiveness, I knew that I'd had false expectations. I knew that forgiveness couldn't override free will. Jesus tells the disciples pretty plainly that "if he doesn't listen" is a real possibility.

Here's what I learned to be true: relationships are not automatically restored by forgiveness.

This was not a happy time for me, realizing that I couldn't miraculously make other people do what I wanted, by waving the magic wand of forgiveness. As I examined the false expectations I had, faced up to the reality of free will, and thought about what made a restored relationship possible, this seemed to be real and true:

A restored relationship requires three separate components: forgiveness, trust, and healing. These three jobs belong to three different members of the relationship.

FORGIVENESS is simply the pardoning of the debt. Forgiveness first acknowledges that there is a real, true debt. Then forgiveness says, "I let go of my right to the debt I am owed." I freely receive from God, and so I can freely forgive others. Jesus is passionately committed to justice and mercy, he is on my side, and he has more for me than the offender has taken. When I experience those things, I can release the offender from the debt and forgive. This is what the 70 times 7 parable is all about.

From my reading of scripture, forgiveness is clearly my job.

TRUST means that the other person in the relationship behaves in a trustworthy manner, allowing me to honestly trust him. For example, "trustworthy," in our marriage, would mean that when I confronted Andy about his behavior, he would admit his fault and **change**. As he turned away from bad old patterns and created new, healthy patterns he would be trustworthy and reconciliation would be possible. If he didn't change, I would be foolish to trust him.

Trustworthy behavior is the other person's job.

HEALING is the third component. When I forgive, I create a healthy environment for healing in my life. Forgiveness is like cleaning out a wound so healing can begin. I can get the gunk out and put on medicine and a bandage, but the actual closing of the wound takes place over time in a process that I barely understand, much less have control over.

Ultimately, healing is God's job.

Since I'm a visual learner, I came up with a picture of this that made sense to me.

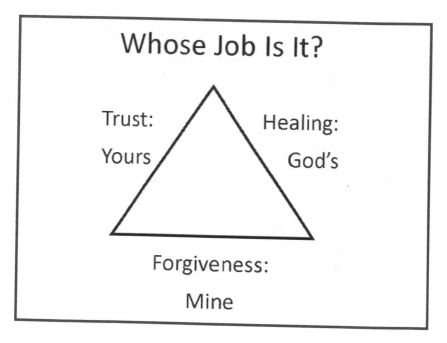

The Restoration Triangle: Forgiveness

I put forgiveness at the bottom of the triangle, because it's impossible to have a restored relationship without forgiveness. God lets me choose whether I want to open the door to healing and restoration, or just live with my indignation forever. I can forgive, or I can hang onto my anger and hatred and live in that prison until I die. Those are really the only two choices, and it's up to me. I choose whether to forgive, or not.

This is forgiveness:

There is an actual debt that should be paid. I choose to release you from that payment.

Forgiveness is NOT saying that it doesn't matter.

Forgiveness is NOT saying that it's no big deal.

Forgiveness is NOT saying that it really doesn't bother me.

Forgiveness is NOT saying that it's all fine now and I'll never have to think about it again.

Forgiveness is NOT saying that the relationship is restored right now.

Forgiveness is NOT saying that I won't have boundaries any more.

Forgiveness says: it's a big deal and it matters and it bothers me.

Forgiveness says: even if I forgive right now, I'll have to wait and see if I can trust you again.

Forgiveness says: I get to choose whether or not I want to be around a person who made terrible choices to hurt me. It might not be the wise thing for me, now or maybe ever.

Forgiveness says: even if I forgive right now, I'm still going to have pain that needs to be healed and worked through.

But forgiveness says: I don't want to live in this prison forever. I want to move on.

Forgiveness says: I release this debt. I let it go.

Most of the time, we're talking about an emotional debt. Emotional debts are difficult to quantify. They're hard to pin down. But they are very real, and very painful. Emotional debts are comprised of failures between parents and children, husbands and wives, friends and companions. In our very closest, most vulnerable relationships, we have not received the consideration, the care, the love, the attention that we desire.

Sometimes we haven't consciously acknowledged or understood the debt. We just keep experiencing painful emotions over and over in various relationships: "I am always overlooked," "Everybody always leaves me," "I'm such a disappointment," "I can't do anything right." Entrenched patterns of painful emotions like this are very often a symptom of deep emotional debts that may have been incurred years ago.

Let's consider, for example, the relationship between parents and children, since this is a place where emotional debts occur early on, and that often sets the stage for pain that drives us all our lives.

In our culture, we are quick to recognize physical or sexual abuse in a family as a legitimate "debt incurred" scenario. Other emotional debts between parents and children, however, are less legitimized. These real but unrecognized emotional debts lead to what I like to call "but my family is a wonderful family" (BMFIAWF) Syndrome.

In BMFIAWF Syndrome, clients enter therapy with deep pain in their hearts, chaos in their closest relationships, and a solid story about how they can't have this pain and this chaos because their family is a wonderful family. I think a lot of BMFIAWF sufferers are afraid that if they confront the debt, they will cause themselves even more pain by disrupting relationships within their families. Ironically, that fear and the unwillingness to acknowledge the debt often leads to an inability to fully release the pain. That's what the symptoms of hurt and chaos are all about. Here are a few examples of things that happen in otherwise wonderful families that incur emotional debt.

> **Maybe our parents fought, and we had to comfort the wounded parent, provide the comic relief, be the successful hero of the family, or operate as the black sheep to distract from the real problem.**

> **Maybe we had a parent with mental illness or a difficult personality, whose issues took up so much space in the family that there wasn't much room for the kids' stuff.**

> **Maybe our families were in ministry/missions/military, so other needs became more important than our own.**

> **Maybe we simply weren't allowed to have our own feelings, opinions, or ideas. We weren't allowed to**

differentiate from our parents.

Maybe we grew up in a religious context that required us to think, feel or behave in ways that were ultimately harmful to our spiritual and emotional health.

Compared to physical or sexual abuse of a child, these issues are, therapeutically speaking, less severe, it's true. There may have been wonderful times together as a family in addition to the painful times.

However, when there is pain, for whatever reason, at whatever level of severity, that pain needs to be healed. If you visit your doctor's office with a sprained ankle, you won't be turned away because you don't have cancer. **Everything, large and small, is worth healing, so that we can live whole and free.**

What's more, God has got plenty of healing available for all of us. The fountain will not run dry. However great or small the debt owed to us, God's mercy and grace is poured out for us. When we minimize our pain, when we refuse to acknowledge the debt, we can't release the debt, and we're discarding a great salvation that's right in front of us for the taking.

Another relationship that very often results in emotional debt is marriage. We all wish that "happily ever after" was a real thing, but it's not. Sometimes we speak those vows, and then find ourselves with a spouse who has serious problems meeting the emotional requirements of marriage. We've already talked about abuse, addiction, and adultery. We know that the assertiveness-and-forgiveness model empowers us to have good boundaries and make healthy decisions. We know that treating a spouse "as a pagan" may sadly result in separation or divorce. We wish that weren't the case, but we live in the real world. We know it happens, and it happens for good reason.

But what about those marriages that don't involve abuse, addiction, or adultery, just a lot of regret? What about those cases where you feel compelled to stay, but you're pretty sure you'll stay hurting and lonely? What about that spouse who can't or won't connect deeply and truly? What about that grinding disappointment of a marriage that never adds up to the emotional intimacy that we all long for and legitimately need? What about *that* kind of debt that will never get paid?

For all that anguish, there is healing and hope as well, I believe. I do believe that forgiveness is part of the path toward personal healing in those deeply difficult relationships. It's a process, though. I don't think that's a release you can come to quickly or easily, but I've seen people do it. I think you'll need a good therapist and loving arms around you as you walk that out, and you'll need safe people to hang with you as you continue to walk that out. But I do believe that kind of forgiveness-release is absolutely possible when we turn toward the height, the length, the breadth, the depth of the Love that never lets us go. (Ephesians 3) I've seen God provide the emotional needs lacking in the marriage relationship through loving friends, and through God's own "peace that passes understanding." (Philippians 4:7)

When we are secure in Love, and calm in our spirits, we can then make healthy decisions about how the relationship needs to look. Do we hang on? Do we release it? Those are choices I think we can only make honestly when we're truly safe in Love, and I think forgiveness can help bring us to that place of shelter.

Forgiveness starts with acknowledging emotional debts, even if they occurred in a wonderful family, even if they are ongoing in a marriage that breaks our hearts. That means telling the full story of what happened, what continues to happen, and how that impacted us in the past and in the present. Just like an audit reveals the financial status of an institution, telling the story reveals the emotional status of our debt. Telling the story may mean journaling, talking to a trusted friend, meeting with a therapist. We're not telling the story to blame and to gossip and to get people on our side. *We're telling the story to acknowledge the debt, so that we can release (forgive) it.*

Acknowledging the debt can take time, maybe months or even years. We may have the intention to forgive, and be in the process of forgiveness, long before we have finally forgiven. Some debts are just that big. Some pain is just that deep.

As we forgive, we're always, in our hearts, clinging to the fact that God loves us and has us safe, this whole time. No matter how vast the debt, no matter how profound the hurt, we can go into that darkness knowing that God will hold us close and walk us through. Ultimately, because of God's great wealth of Love for us, we're going to be able to let this debt go.

In a teeny tiny nutshell, forgiveness goes like this:

"I acknowledge the debt that you owe me, and the pain it has caused."

"Because God meets my needs, I am whole, complete, safe, and beloved."

"I choose to release you from your debt."

In reality, though, forgiveness doesn't fit into a nutshell. And drawing forgiveness as a straight line on one side of a triangle is misleading, too. The whole thing should probably look more like this:

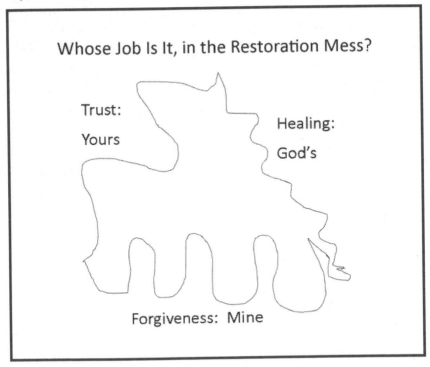

Whose Job Is It, in the Restoration Mess?

Trust: Yours

Healing: God's

Forgiveness: Mine

The process of acknowledging the debt and the pain is messy and difficult and time-consuming. But, I think that as long as I'm doing my best to release the person, then I'm doing my part. I believe that while I am doing my job, forgiving, that God is at work, healing. I don't think God waits until I have perfect understanding and perfect peace about the situation before He is willing to heal. I think my willingness to forgive is all the invitation He needs to start healing.

Reflect

What is the debt? What is the impact of this debt on my life?

What is missing from my life as a result of that debt?

What have I had to deal with as a result of that debt?

Who knows the story of this debt?

Who will lovingly listen to me recount this story, as a part of the forgiveness process?

What keeps me from telling the story of this debt?

What anxiety or fear comes up for me when I think about telling this story?

The Restoration Triangle: Trust

Here's a little manifesto about trust, from the victim to the offender.

Forgiveness is free, trust is earned.

Forgiveness is free--it's my gift to you.

Trust is earned, as I observe your trustworthy behavior over time.

That may sound harsh, but this is the real world.

God can see your heart. All I can see is your behavior.

And, even if you are trustworthy, I still get to choose what kind of relationship I'd like to have with you in the future. Let me say that again.

Even if you are trustworthy, I still get to choose what kind of relationship I'd like to have with you in the future.

You can't demand trust. You can't demand relationship. When you've hurt me, all you can do is be trustworthy, continue to be trustworthy, and wait.

To demand that I hurry up and trust you again is not trustworthy.

Being sorry for a little while and then going back to old behavior is not trustworthy.

Blaming or shaming me for being hurt about your behavior is not trustworthy.

I grew up with Charlie Brown comics. Charlie Brown liked kicking a football, but in order to kick the football, he needed somebody to hold it for him. Inevitably, his so-called friend, Lucy, would hold the ball while Charlie Brown came running. At the last second, she'd pull the ball away and Charlie Brown would fall on his head. This same scenario happened over and over between Charlie Brown and Lucy.

In my opinion, Charlie Brown was making a huge mistake in judgment, trusting Lucy over and over again. Her behavior was simply not trustworthy. Charlie Brown had other options, though. He could have walked away. He could have found somebody else to hold his football. He could have gotten one of those little plastic football-holder doo-hickeys. He could have switched to a soccer ball, for Pete's sake. There were tons of ways to disengage from Lucy's untrustworthy behavior. But, no. There he was, over and over and over, with his big round head smack on the pavement again and Lucy grinning like a maniac above him. It was just painful to watch.

Restoration of the relationship is only possible if the wrong-doer changes, and becomes trustworthy. In fancy church words, we call that *repentance*. Repentance is much more than saying, "I'm sorry." Real repentance goes far beyond words. Real repentance means that the offender will *stop the behavior* and *work on the underlying issues* that caused the behavior.

She might get an accountability system in place. She might go to therapy or a 12-step group. In addition, real repentance means that the offender will make amends for any of the consequences of her behavior. Lucy might pay the hospital bill for Charlie Brown's multiple concussions.

But real trustworthiness enters a huge territory that I'm not sure Lucy is capable of: empathy. Dr. John Gottman is one of the world's foremost experts on healthy marriage relationships, and he has some interesting things to say about trust. According to Gottman, trust means far more than having dependable and honest behavior. Good behavior, and the practical trust that comes with it, is wonderful and necessary in a healthy relationship. What really builds the strength and depth of the relationship, though, is emotionally trustworthiness. Being emotionally trustworthy means that you *genuinely care about how the other person feels, and you demonstrate that caring in practical ways.*

Gottman says that we constantly have opportunities to build emotional trust. We do that in small moments when we connect with our partners by caring about how they feel right then. Sometimes we're just too busy or tired to pay attention to our partners, and we turn away emotionally. The sad reality is: it's hard work to emotionally connect with each other sometimes. It's easier to watch TV than it is to emotionally turn toward our partners. And, truthfully, a few isolated incidents of turning away from connection are not all that critical. But when a partner constantly chooses to turn away, then over time, trust erodes. It's such an incremental process—turning toward, turning away--that it's hard to pinpoint. But those small turns—toward or away--are critical over time to the trust state of the relationship.

A lot of times in therapy, we'll have couples with a "good

person," who is an innocent bystander, and a "bad person", who has done whatever they did. Usually the problems have been going on for a while before the couple comes to therapy; in fact, therapy is often a last resort. The "bad person" stops doing the bad thing, because they realize that the marriage is on its last legs. And then the "bad person" expects the "good person" to immediately trust again. The "good person," however, feels manipulated and doesn't think it's real. And I usually agree.

The missing element in that scenario (besides time and repeated trustworthy behavior) is *emotional trust.* A person who really, truly repents will really, truly care about the other person's experience and emotions. The offender will understand that he has done deep damage, and that damage takes time to heal. He won't be upset and impatient and demanding of the person who's trying to heal. He won't build a case about how fabulous his recovery process is and how everybody else thinks he's fantastic, and demand that his victim get on board the love train. In fact, the total opposite. He will want to listen and empathize and make amends whenever possible. He will be humble and gentle and quiet and patient with the person he has wounded. If necessary, he will accept that he has damaged the relationship beyond repair and he will grieve that loss as part of his own recovery process.

Turning toward the relationship doesn't mean we have to agree with each other 100% all the time. In fact, one of the things Dr. Gottman points out in his research is that all couples, including happy ones, have ongoing, unresolved disagreements. The difference between unhappy and happy couples around those disagreements is this element of turning toward: being attuned to the other person's emotions, and being committed to empathy, even when there are disagreements.

Turning toward the relationship means:

Paying attention to how the other person feels,

Inviting them to share those feelings, and

Listening to those feelings without dismissing, disregarding, denying or being defensive.

Being able to sit with another person's feelings without doing anything but listening and caring is not a skill that most of us have learned, honestly. We might be good at fixing problems or explaining them away or arguing our side of an issue or shooting out a Bible verse that should make it all go away. Most of us, though, don't know how to just listen and care about the other person without telling them what to do or how they don't really need to feel so bad to begin with.

However, emotional trustworthiness requires us to acquire the skill of listening with no agenda apart from understanding and loving the other person. For some basic ideas, I suggest watching this short video by Dr. Gottman. [2]

Even if the offender does repent, even if he does become emotionally trustworthy, even if the relationship is on the way to restoration, the relationship is probably going to look like a mess for a while. Like they say in Alcoholics Anonymous, relapse is part of recovery. The person who's working to establish trust may not have perfect behavior all the time. What I've found for myself, though, is that when the emotional trust is strong, when we are both consistently turning toward the relationship rather than away, I can put up with some imperfect behavior when it's relapse as part of the recovery process.

In a nutshell, here's what it takes for the offender to become trustworthy:

Recognize the offense

Take responsibility for consequences

Repent (change)

Make amends

Consistently behave in trustworthy ways

Consistently turn toward the relationship emotionally

Repeat trustworthy behavior over time

Just as the offender needs to release his demands on me, so I, too, need to release my demands on him to be sorry and change and grow and be trustworthy again.

When we truly release the debt, we will allow the other person to exercise their own free will. When I forgive, the other person is completely free of any demands from me. Their trustworthy behavior and trustworthy emotional connection will come—or not--as a result of their own choices.

It is often very difficult for us to let go of trying to force restoration onto the relationship, but this is what real forgiveness does: it releases. Forgiveness releases and faces the possibility that others may continue to make choices that make restoration impossible.

When real repentance happens, when real trust grows in an atmosphere of emotional caring and connection, then reconciliation and restoration of the relationship is a *possibility*. Remember, the offended person still gets to choose how the relationship will look in the future. **Trustworthy behavior allows for the *possibility* of restoration. It is not a *guarantee*.**

There are cases—probably lots of them--where a reconciled relationship is not possible or desirable. The closest relationships require the most trust, and the most trustworthiness. When that trustworthiness is deeply compromised, as in abuse or addiction, the relationship often does not survive. Here's the sad reality of the real world we live in: forgiveness is not a magic wand. Sometimes the damage is just too great.

However, *even when we don't get the restored relationship we had hoped for,* God can restore our souls as we continue to leave our debts in His hands and invite Him to heal. Our ability or inability to "do forgiveness" or to "do repentance" or to "do reconciliation" perfectly does not undermine God's ability to work for our good.

We may be totally out of options, but God never is.

Reflect

Is the offender's behavior trustworthy?

Does the offender empathize with my emotions?

Is the offender emotionally trustworthy?

Is the offender making demands of me, or being patient and trustworthy?

How can I release this person from my demands, and allow them the exercise of their own free will?

The Restoration Triangle: Healing

Years ago, when we lived in the Solomon Islands, a friend of mine had a miscarriage, followed by a D&C at the local hospital. I was sitting with her just after the surgery, and she kept asking me, over and over, "Why do I feel so horrible?" "Well," I said, "a horrible thing has happened."

I think we can understand, pretty easily, that in the physical realm, injuries take time to heal. We don't expect the guy who got hit by a train today to get up and do the Macarena tomorrow. But it seems like we do expect ourselves to be just that resilient in the emotional realm, and I think that's just plain silly. When we've had a major emotional trauma, it's going to take time to heal.

Even though it takes time, we can expect healing to come. Healing is natural. It's how we're made: created to heal. And while I can't make the edges of a wound bind together,

I can create an environment that aids healing by cleaning the wound, bandaging it, and taking care of it while it heals. I can orient myself toward healing, by keeping my mind and heart turned toward forgiveness rather than revenge:

"I refuse to let bitterness grow in me."

"I bring my pain to God and trust him to heal me in time."

"I accept the new joy, peace, and rest that God wants to give me."

The actual work of healing is God's job. I don't need to feel bad about being in pain, and I don't have to worry about what makes the healing happen. I simply turn toward healing, rest, and let it come.

A while back, I read somewhere that we are created like trees, to grow. Of course, if we're trapped under a giant bolder of bitterness, resentment, and revenge, it's hard for the healing and growth to happen.

And so, by the act of forgiveness, we roll the stone away and open ourselves to the sunlight, to the rain, to the natural goodness of Love. When we do that, Love seeps down into our souls to heal and to restore, to build and to grow.

Whenever I get lost in the process of healing and I start to get upset with the person again, thinking of what they owe me, I turn back toward Love, and experience again that Love is enough. Whenever I get lost or confused in the process of healing, I turn toward Love.

Over and over and over again, I turn to Love.

And Love keeps on healing.

When I think of all this, I fall to my knees and pray to the Father, the Creator of everything in heaven and on earth. I pray that from his glorious, unlimited resources he will empower you with inner strength through his Spirit. Then Christ will make his home in your hearts as you trust in him. Your roots will grow down into God's love and keep you strong. And may you have the power to understand, as all God's people should, how wide, how long, how high, and how deep his love is. May you experience the love of Christ, though it is too great to understand fully. Then you will be made complete with all the fullness of life and power that comes from God.

Ephesians 3:14-19 NLT

Reflect

What stands in the way of healing in my life?

How difficult is it for me to rest and wait for healing?

What do I expect healing to look like in my life?

What will be different for me, when I am healed?

The Restoration Triangle

Trust: Yours*

To rebuild trust, the offender must:
Recognize the offense
Take responsibility for consequences
Repent (change)
Repeat trustworthy behavior

Healing: God's

"I refuse to let bitterness grow in me."
"I bring my pain to God and trust him to heal me in time."
"I accept the new joy, peace, and rest that God wants to give me."

When I refuse to forgive, I refuse healing.

Forgiveness: Mine

"I acknowledge the debt that you owe me, and the pain it has caused."
"Because God meets my needs, I am whole, complete, safe, and beloved."
"I choose to release you from your debt."

Because God loves me, I have more than enough.
I no longer need what the offender holds.
I forgive the debt.
I bring my pain and grief to God and trust him to heal me.
I accept the freedom, life, joy, peace, and rest that are waiting for me.

The offender may remain an unsafe person for me. If this is the case, I will need to grieve the loss of this relationship and ask God to bring safe people into my life. With these safe people, I can build new trust relationships, and continue to allow God to heal me.

Kay Bruner 2009

Myth #6: Forgiveness requires restoration of the relationship

Many of us have been taught that forgiveness means the relationship must be restored, no matter what. That's what we've been told 70 times 7 means: restored relationship, open to whatever that other person wants to do, no matter how many times they want to do it.

Of course, we know now that this view totally overlooks Jesus' teachings on assertiveness and confrontation. Remember, "let him be treated as a pagan" is what happens to people who refuse to repent.

That brings us to this last difficult question: what if the other person never repents? What if she is never trustworthy again? What happens to the relationship then?

I think that in those cases, we release the relationship.

We might need to release friends who take and take and take and never give.

We might need to release a beloved organization or a church that takes a turn for the worse and can't find its way back.

We might need to release parents whose own emotional pain keeps them from connecting as we hope.

We might need to release siblings who just can't seem to let go of the past.

We might need to release a spouse who is lost in addiction or abuse.

When we release an important relationship, there are two courses of action we can choose from.

First, we may continue to have regular contact with that person, but *we stop expecting that person to meet the emotional responsibility of the relationship.* We let that expectation go.

Second, we might choose to have very little or no contact with the person. If the person has been abusive, this is often a wise choice.

We might start out thinking that regular contact is okay, only to find ourselves being abused and needing to re-evaluate how much contact we can handle.

There is no single right way to "do release." We simply make the best choice we can, with the information we have now, and trust God for the rest.

We accept the reality that this person is unable to be trustworthy for us. We grieve that loss, we feel that pain.

Releasing is a sad, painful, and difficult task. While it may bring relief eventually, releasing a relationship often creates its own world of hurt. When we rip off the bandage of denial, the truth of our hurt and disappointment can be agonizing. In the midst of that pain, the wealth of God's love and care for us can seem like a mirage created by a madman.

Many times we participate in the myths of forgiveness,

spinning through a prolonged and impossible process that never results in healing or change, specifically to protect ourselves from letting go. We've built and sustained this forgiveness-myth monster to keep an even bigger monster at bay: grief.

But we can do hard things, right? And so, at last, we unclench our fists and we let it go.

And this is what we find to be true: Love works for healing in our lives even if those relationships are never restored.

As we release, we create space hearts for others who can be trustworthy for us.

We trust that God will continue to be at work in that other person's life, even when we can't.

Releasing the relationship doesn't mean that we shun or hate or despise. We simply release the other person from our expectations and obligations, and trust God to bless that other person. I may not have the capacity, in my pain, to be a blessing to that person. But God can, and He will. No matter how badly the relationship may have ended, God still loves that person. He loves me. As we release relationships, we trust that God redeems and restores, even though we can't.

One of the things we may face, as we release relationships, is judgment from others who insist on reconciliation, no matter what. The truth is, a lot of people still think forgiveness is that easy-peasy IKEA floor model, and they want us to slap it together as fast as we can, and be done with it.

If that works for them, fine. We've come to realize, how-ever, that there are deeper issues at stake for us, and we're working through them differently than others might do. Those people have free will. We have free will. We are each responsible to God for the choices we make.

When we find ourselves facing that kind of pressure, here are some steps to take:

> **Remember that assertiveness and forgiveness go hand-in-hand.**
>
> **Remember that we can't control the other person; they have a right to their ideas. They have their own free will to live with, and we have ours.**
>
> **Remember that Jesus comes to bring rest for our souls, not to weigh us down with more burdens.**
>
> **Choose our boundaries and hold them confidently.**
>
> **Be willing to release those who are judging us. They may owe us a debt of support and under-standing that they are unable to provide. We've learned, however, how to forgive those who can't help us, and to receive what we need from God instead. The person who insists on reconciliation may be just another opportunity for us to forgive and release, to live free and clear.**

Reflect

Is there a relationship I need to release?

What can I do to let that person go?

What will that relationship look like, when I have released that person?

How much contact seems wise to me right now?

Where will I turn for support as I process the pain of releasing that relationship?

The power of forgiveness, repentance, and healing

In October 2010, CBS News ran a story entitled "The Power of Forgiveness." As I watched that story for the first time just recently, I realized that it's a perfect demonstration of what happens when the Restoration Triangle works out in real life. If CBS News had asked me, I would have suggested that they call it "The Power of Forgiveness, Repentance, and Healing." It is the story of the "remarkable mercy" of Mary Johnson, whose 20-year-old son, her only child, was shot dead at a party in 1993. His 16-year-old killer, Oshay Israel, was convicted of the murder and served 17 years in prison. During Oshay's time in prison, Mary, a committed Christian, decided to visit her son's killer, to see if she could forgive him. [3]

As a mother of three young adult sons, I can't imagine the pain Mary suffered at the loss of her only son. The courage of her convictions and her faith to follow Jesus into forgiveness just blows me away.

But that's what she did. She visited Oshay in prison, and she forgave him. She forgave him so much that when he was released, she introduced him to her landlord, and he moved in next door.

And Oshay repented. You can see it on his face, and in the way he talks about how hard it is for him to accept forgiveness for what he did.

And there's healing. You can see that in the way the two of them speak to groups together, about faith and forgiveness.

Here's what Mary has to say about it all:

"Unforgiveness is like cancer. It will eat you from the inside out. It's not about that other person. Me forgiving him does not diminish what he's done. Yes, he murdered my son. But forgiveness is for me. It's for me."

Doesn't that sound exactly like rest for all our weary souls?

Doesn't that sound like freedom for prisoners and recovery of sight for the blind?

Forgiveness is not a heavy burden designed to weigh us down when we're already half-dead with pain.

Forgiveness is the gift of spiritual abundance that breaks our chains, sets us free, and sparks a new life of healing, grace, growth, and peace.

Resources for further study

Boundaries, Henry Cloud and John Townsend

Forgiving the Dead Man Walking, Debbie Morris

The Book of Forgiving, Desmond Tutu and Mpho Tutu

Transitions, William Bridges

References

1.http://www.pbs.org/wgbh/pages/frontline/shows/religion/portrait/jews.html

2. http://www.youtube.com/watch?v=rgWnadSi91s)

3. https://www.youtube.com/watch?v=o2BITY-3Mp4

54742886R00045

Made in the USA
Charleston, SC
11 April 2016